HOW INTREPID THE DISABLED KITTEN

TRIUMPHED TO HELP OTHERS

Signe A. Dayhoff, PhD

How Intrepid the Disabled Kitten
Triumphed to Help Others
by Signe A. Dayhoff, PhD

Copyright © 2016 by Signe A. Dayhoff, PhD
Published by Effectiveness-Plus Publications LLC
80 Paseo de San Antonio
Placitas, New Mexico 87043-8735

Cover photo by Signe A. Dayhoff
Cover design by around86 at fiverr.com

ISBN: 978-0-9970168-0-2

PUBLISHER'S NOTE

DEDICATION

This book is dedicated to professionals and volunteers who help rescue, trap-neuter-and-return, and care for all homeless animals, but especially for cats. It is dedicated to all those compassionate, empathetic veterinary professionals, like Dr. George Abernathy at Sunrise Animal Clinic, in Rio Rancho, NM, and his committed veterinary technicians who work hard together to help ferry these ill or injured homeless animals back from the brink of death so they can live more functional, loving, and protected lives.

This book is also dedicated to the cat who generously gave his permission to Dr. Dayhoff to transcribe and share his story of going from developmental disability and the dangers of homelessness to the warm protection of living in a home with a caring human and sharing himself with others. In spite of all he has gone through, he remains the small, handsome, street-wise, and super-sweet kitty who continues to act as a reminder of what professionals and volunteers can do when they work together to save all homeless animals, no matter what their challenges.

TABLE OF CONTENTS

1

STRUGGLING IN NM WINTERS

Figuring out how to keep warm in winters in central New Mexico, where temperatures can plunge to 15 degrees with 30-mph winds from the east, can be a real challenge for *any* sentient being living on the streets. Unlike homeless humans, homeless cats like me don't have organized shelters where we may be able to grab a night's safe, warm lodging.

Can you imagine the Salvation Army, or any other rescue mission, having a separate room with wall-to-wall kitty beds decorating the floor (as well as more than a few litter pans) to address our winter survival needs too? I wish but I guess they can do only so much and their first priority is, after all, homeless people. *Homo sapiens* do tend to come first in most people's charitable consideration and actions, which I guess is reasonable. Still—

As a result, we felines without homes have to be constantly creative about finding the right protection at the right time in order to survive. And, sadly, too many of us don't.

Before I go on, I ought to introduce myself. I am a young, diminutive, slightly shy but sweet-dispositioned male cat. As humans would point out, I also walk a little funny and have difficulty judging distance. When I'm nervous, excited, or focusing on something, my head shakes a little. But in spite of that, which I don't consider a big deal, I've gotten by.

I don't know how I've remained so pleasant and positive considering all I've been through. I was born to a homeless mother in a felled, rot-hollowed-out cottonwood tree in the farmland of Corrales. Mice were in abundance most of that year but she had to work hard to catch enough of the savvy little creatures to keep us both fed. There were no kitty kibbutzim around the area. Consequently, we had only ourselves to rely on in our food gathering efforts. Because I was a little uncoordinated I wasn't as much help as I could have been.

At the end of summer two years ago, my beloved mother was still in the process of teaching me how to hunt. I would never have imagined it. Wobbly me acting like a macho cat? Oh, boy! She showed me how to lurk, quietly, not moving a whisker. Once I almost had that down, she went on to pouncing and catching. It was more like tumbling and landing on top of the mouse.

Executing the so-called "death grip" on prey required a lot of practice. I started with grasshoppers—which was truly disgusting. Their wings are leathery and unyielding and their back legs have saw-like teeth. And if I happened to puncture its abdomen even slightly on the rare times I caught them, the taste was grotesque.

When I upgraded to mice, grabbing onto their furry little necks was supposed to be easier. I still hadn't mastered the steel-trap grip so most of my subjects, when I could actually catch them, quickly extricated themselves. They were a little soggy but unscathed. My mother repeatedly reminded me that anything worth doing well takes time. I would have a lot more practicing to do before I could become somewhat proficient and hopefully self-sustaining.

Our regular practice field was at a distance, across Loma Larga Road. My mother seemed to think that the more walking I did, the stronger and more coordinated I'd become. My head bobbing and limb tremors didn't bother me all that much except that I didn't walk or run as smoothly as I'd have liked, especially when following her. She was very patient with me.

When we arrived at Loma Larga, as usual my mother checked the traffic both ways before we started across. All was clear. But only about four or five feet onto the road, the inconceivable happened. A speeding red GMC pickup truck materialized out of nowhere. Seven thousand pounds propelled by a V8 engine were bearing down on us.

My mother who had already reached the center line, turned to shove me out of harm's way. Because I was trailing behind her, the truck struck her alone. With a grinding crunch, it flipped her body onto the outer edge of the right lane. Whether or not the driver was aware of what it had done, that human merely sped on. My mother lay crumbled, broken on the edge of the road in paralyzing agony.

For a total of ten hours she lay there without any assistance except my meager, inadequate attempts to comfort her. As only a child knows, I was sure she could have been helped during that time—maybe even have survived the impact—if only some human had ... She deserved that chance.

Something didn't make any sense to me. She had taught me that humans helped. But where was that help as she lay there? All sorts of vehicles went past us but no one stopped. And I had no idea what I could do to make them stop. I was too young to do much more than cuddle with her, my trembling paws covering her body. At least, perhaps, I could keep her safe from further attacks.

Down in the depth of my being I cringed. I knew that her condition was really my fault. She had been crossing the street for me, to teach me what I needed to know. Then she had thrown herself into the truck's path to save me.

My mother had told me of the many humans who lived in the village of Corrales. Among them there was an abundance of animal people who were caring and compassionate. That initially made me confident someone would stop and save my mother for me. But as she and I lay barely several inches on the asphalt, cars went around us. Some honked at us as if we were lying there unaware, and once startled by the imminent danger, would immediately pick up and move.

While they may have thought they were being caring and helpful by trying to get us off the road so we wouldn't get splattered, they weren't. Making invalid assumptions, they alerted us then went passively on their way. They never stopped to actually determine what the situation really was. It all made the pain in my heart that much worse. It didn't occur to me at the time that our bodies hunkered together like that may have looked already dead, un-rescuable. But no one checked!

As a result, no one but me paid her the respect she deserved even after she finally died either. I wanted someone to carefully move her body from the side of the road to the shoulder. No one volunteered. I'd have to do it ... somehow. But then I wanted someone to do something more for her, something appropriate. But what would be appropriate? I had no idea.

Burying her body was out of the question. Being placed in a hole and covered with dirt did not sit right with me. Cats buried their waste, not their loved ones. I'd heard horror stories about deceased cats being tossed into a dumpster or onto some dead animal pile behind a veterinary clinic. That was so disrespectful. And if she was simply left by the side of the road, scavengers of different species would feast on her body. That was too repulsive to contemplate.

I was so confused and conflicted. She deserved a dignified sendoff. She deserved to be respected in death as well as in life. She was my mother, not just a hunk of dead flesh. A simple plan began to come together in my mind. Before I could do anything else I'd first have to address removing her from the road.

After a few close calls with vehicles as I tried to push her further off the road surface, it became clear I was putting myself at risk with my rear end in the road. It would have been insulting to my mother to allow myself to become another traffic statistic as I did this. She had taught me about road hazards and avoiding them. Consequently, she expected so much more of me. I *could not—would not*—leave her where she was. But I certainly couldn't let her down either. I owed her.

Despite my youth and constant disequilibrium, I reversed course. Using my teeth and all the strength I possessed, I stood off the road and tugged at her lifeless body. She seemed inordinately heavy. Even so, I stayed with her. With maximum frustration I was only minimally successful, sometimes only managing to re-orient her body. Between passing cars and trucks, I anxiously experimented with different positions of my wide-based legs and where I grabbed her. Two days of systematic pulling finally completed that task.

Once I had her resting on the shoulder of the road among some young green Russian thistle shoots—the same invasive weed that when dry is called tumbleweed—I knew logically I had to leave her. I had been days without food and water since her accident. But now I had to do something with her body. How comforting it would have been to be able to have placed her in the quiet shadow of an ancient cottonwood. Its meditatively musical leaves would softly mimic the tinkle of a small stream lazily running over river rocks when a breeze blew. But that was a fantasy. Due to area development, there were no nearby cottonwoods.

I didn't want to accept that she was beyond my further assistance. I felt I should continue to be there for her. So I stayed with her beside the road for the rest of the day. But I knew I had to leave her. Bereft, depressed, and embittered, I finally pushed myself to embark on my own solitary struggle to survive. Still, in spite of the grim reality of my own situation, I recognized that the guilt about abandoning her would never leave me.

My mother was truly beautiful, but I guess most mothers are seen that way by their kittens. She was graced with pale green eyes, sort of like pistachio ice cream I'd seen children licking on sugar cones, a long black coat she somehow kept clean and neat, and a luxurious plume-like tail which swayed seductively as she walked. If any cat belonged in a caring household where she could sit in the window and soak up the solars and enjoy regular meals and loads of attention, she did.

To me she was a paragon, every bit as tough, practical, kind, and gentle as she was beautiful. If humans could, and would, emulate only one quality of hers, they would be so much more worthy beings for it.

Alas, I can't say I really look much like her. From a distance my long-haired coat, which I manage well considering, looks black too but is really smoke-colored. That is, I have guard hairs that are long, black, and glossy. Most exposed to the elements, they shed water, block sunlight, and protect the undercoat and skin from ultraviolet. However, my undercoat, which is more down-like, varies in shades from black to gray to silver—something like an East Asian ink wash painting. To put it poetically, as I am occasionally wont to do, my eyes look like thyme honey oozing from a honeycomb, glinting in the summer sun.

2

FINDING SAFE SHELTER

As for finding shelter in bad or cold weather, I've tried just about every opening, crack, crevice, hole, niche, or human-made structure I could locate in my travels around the neighborhoods west of Interstate 25. That includes discarded cardboard boxes, toppled trash containers, abandoned and rusting vehicles, stoves, refrigerators, microwaves, barns, covered lawn furniture, lean-tos, and woodpiles. As you might guess, woodpiles are the least desirable. Besides being difficult to navigate, they are also the refuge for rats, mice, snakes, and raccoons, not to mention spiders of every ilk, particularly black widows who favor such dark places. However, sometimes one has no choice.

Uncountable months had passed since my mother's demise. I was getting bigger, older, and hopefully smarter. At the end of one of my travels for sustenance and shelter, where I had received handouts from humans who awaited my daily arrival, I spotted a small gray lump on the muddy side of the road. At closer inspection, I saw it was a kitten that had gotten it paws stuck. I made an attempt to grab it by the scruff of its neck, trying to duplicate my mother's kitten-carrying technique. It took a while to get a solid grip.

Then I jostled it back and forth, tumbling once or twice, until I extricated it—with a plop. As the tiny kitten hung from my jaws, I realized I had a problem. Now what was I to do with it? I wondered. In a way I felt I wasn't much older than it was. But the sun was setting and this little one needed assistance.

Surveilling the area, I saw no open outbuildings. But I did spot a loosely-packed woodpile near what looked like an old farm house about fifty feet away. With trepidation I headed us in that direction. The kitten swayed precariously as I waddled toward the logs, dragging its butt over the brown grasses and weed stubble poking through the snow. Sorry, kit, I empathized, hoping I wasn't injuring him as I tried to save him.

It took a long time before we reached the farmhouse. A lavender twilight was upon us and shadows were deepening. The log pile looked menacing. Despite my considerable distaste, I managed to wedge the kitten's small body into a gap which I considered a little too tight for my liking. A half an hour later I had squeezed my body in around the kitten. As we hunkered down, the kitten firmly curled between my front paws. Until the next morning, its high metabolism helped keep me warmer too. At least as I dozed off, my tremors subsided.

Tomorrow morning I realized I had a big problem. I was no longer looking for food for one. I had a kitten with a big appetite to feed as well. What do kittens eat? What did I eat at that age? Mice? As the sun rolled over the Sandia Mountains to saturate all the colors of

Nature, the kitten was still snoring softly. To look around, outside the woodpile, I'd have to move it. Not just yet. Let me work this out first.

Maybe I could get the attention of humans at the farmhouse and present this baby to them. They couldn't refuse this helpless baby and would take it in. I didn't hold out any hope they would feel the same about a twitching adolescent who lists to one side.

Just as I was about to slide out backwards from among the logs, I heard a cat walking slowly past the other side of the woodpile, meowing. Concern tinged the calling. Awakened, the kitten mewled in response. The cat excitedly sought out its source. Pushing the gray kitten around the logs toward the adult, I waited with bated breath. As the kitten poked its head out, the adult delicately pulled it all the way to the ground. I couldn't believe it. Apparently the cat was the kitten's mother.

After a few licks and running her paws over the kitten's coat, she likewise grabbed the mud-splotched baby by the scruff of the neck—much more expertly than I—and turned toward the house. She carried it with confidence and satisfaction. Exiting the woodpile as quickly and quietly as my tremors would allow, I thought I might be able to take advantage of this opportunity.

Unfortunately, I wasn't silent enough. Startled, the mama cat whirled around just before she reached the back door. Unceremoniously she dropped the gray fluff bundle on the packed snow and faced me. Her ears were back, her bushed-out tail raised high above her arched back. There was no mistaking the ferocity of the hiss she shot at me. I was encroaching on her territory as well as threatening her kitten.

When aggression won't help, be submissive. I flopped over on my side to show I had no ill intentions. She watched me for a while mesmerized by my constant movement before scooping up her kitten again. Slowly she ascended the two steps to the back door, warily keeping an eye on me, then scratched on the weathered wood to be let in. On my feet again, I moved cautiously toward the steps. As the mama and baby disappeared inside, I began to call. Maybe the human would take pity on me and give me something to stave my hunger.

The door closed. Should I continue to make my presence known? Should I put my dignity aside and grovel? You can't eat dignity. Resigned, I prostrated myself. I voiced my sincerest hope that because they were obviously cat people they would help out a feline in need. I waited. Nothing happened.

Before I could resume I heard the rumble. Chewed ears were coming into view. Several street-tough cats were jockeying for position, glaring at me from behind the chintz-curtained window by the door. Growling and slapping the glass with their large paws, they were obviously neither pleased nor amused by my performance. This was a cold audience. Because of their caterwauling, the human slammed open the back door. She clapped her hands together and shouted, "Go away, you diseased thing! You're upsetting my cats! And don't come back or I'll call Animal Control!" Well, that was that. At least the kitten had lucked out.

I retraced my steps, careful to give the woodpile plenty of room. It was then I finally noticed the gossamer threads of a spider web clinging to my fur. Ooh! My body quivered. There was no question: woodpiles were absolutely the *very* last resort for shelter.

Another possible shelter was the front wheel wells of cars that had been in use. When the vehicle had recently returned from a trip somewhere, the front wheel wells were immediately warm and inviting because of their proximity to the engine. There I didn't have to worry about lots of other animals competing for the same spot. Although on a few occasions another cat and I had words about whose place it *really* was for the night. You can't exactly call for reservations. But, then again, because of their relative exposure to the weather, front wheel wells were not as good as ensconcing oneself on the vehicle's engine block.

Ah, yes, the engine compartment. I have strong recollections of taking advantage of all that glorious heat. In case you don't know, any small animal like me can squeeze into the compartment from under the front end of the car which is amazingly open to any critter that is of a mind to enter. Of course, for someone like me, it's an arduous maneuver to climb in but generally worth it.

Mice and rats in particular relish lodging there where they can also sharpen their teeth gnawing on the wiring harness. Inside the horizontal surface is flatter and wider than a wheel well. I've discovered that the dimensions depend greatly upon the make and model of the car.

However, irrespective of the make and model, that space is often lacking in height. So whether you're my small size or larger or, heaven forbid "claustrophobic," you have to gird your kitty loins, close your eyes, and push through your anxiety to squeeze in. When you're a homeless cat, your options for dealing with unpleasant meteorological events are slim to none. The result? You go with the flow. Besides, it's definitely an improvement over curling up on top of a hard, rapidly-cooling rubber tire.

Another advantage is that the hood keeps that area warm longer. It also protects you from rain, snow, hail, sleet, and wind. Unfortunately, I found out the hard way that bivouacking there does have one *huge* disadvantage.

After shoehorning myself into the engine compartment of a dark blue Ford sedan which was parked in a gravel driveway on my route, I settled in and fell asleep quickly. Throughout the night, however, I heard icy snow batter the hood like discharged shotgun pellets. It repeatedly startled me wide awake. The next morning a full-blown blizzard greeted me outside. Looking down, I could see past the engine to observe the wind swirling and pushing heavy snow around the front wheels. I had no real desire to leave my still-cozy quarters to do my uncoordinated slog through the storm to start on my food scrounging rounds.

Consequently, I waited a tad too long to leave. I was feeling sleepy and a little lazy given the precipitation. Besides, my mother hadn't had a chance to teach me about this aspect of cars, but even if she had—. In the meantime, unbeknownst to me, a human had opened the driver's door. I heard but didn't understand the implications of it. When the ignition switched on and the engine roared to life, I did.

My high-pitched, full-throated scream of exquisite pain instantly echoed throughout the vehicle. The engine immediately ceased. Next the human quickly alighted and threw up the hood. But it was too late. He was greeted with the crimson scenario from "Texas Chainsaw Massacre."

3

CRAWLING INTO DANGER

Blood and tissue glistened everywhere, including the underside of the hood which was dripping onto the engine, the fan and alternator belts, and into the radiator. My left back foot, having lain on the fan belt, had been partially sheared off, looking like a peeled pomegranate. In all the carnage I lay there splattered, sticky wet, and in shock.

The full physical impact of the damage to my ankle and what was left of my foot hadn't as yet registered in my brain. Or maybe endorphins were doing a smashing job of masking the pain. Somehow, in spite of the trauma, my survival instinct clicked in. Reflexively I attempted to leap out of the engine compartment. But my flailing front paws slowed my exit into the now-white driveway. As soon as my body slapped the accumulation with a soft splat, I knew I had to develop a plan ASAP. Unfortunately, nothing appeared on the horizon.

In retrospect I have to admit that despite the seriousness of my injury, previously I had been incredibly lucky. I hate to use that word. "Lucky" would have been not having been born with neurological damage, being homeless in the first place, or having been sliced and diced at all in the second.

However, I'd heard that most cats who were caught under the hood when the engine fired up were killed outright or damaged significantly more than I was. One cat became well-known because his face was almost totally ripped off, requiring a lot of surgery to re-attach it successfully.

As I gathered my wits about me, I started to move out as fast as I could, given my condition and injury. Skittering across the street, I was leaving a trail of blood. While I still couldn't yet feel my foot, I could sense the warm blood pulsing out of me, melting small scarlet holes in the white precipitate beneath it.

I paused to look back. The human was standing by his car in a fog. It was as if he were glued to the spot like a Northwest Pacific Coast Totem Pole, seeing but unseeing. His head and shoulders were gradually being cloaked in icy crystals. It was as if he were trying to decide what to do and not making much headway.

I could envision him thinking, weighing possibilities, such as, what if he went after me? He would likely get all bloody. Maybe in my panic and pain I might bite and scratch him for his efforts. What diseases might he contract as a result? And what would he do if he caught me? He'd have to take me to a vet. What vet? Where?

All that meant he would have to be able to keep me restrained in his car. How would he do that? Not with a seat belt. And I was sure to try to escape. Perhaps I'd leap all over him as he was driving causing him to run off the road. I would definitely bleed all over his tan fabric upholstery in the process. And, perhaps most importantly, what would be his reward for being a Good Samaritan? He'd be covered in blood, maybe have a dented fender, be late for work, and have a large vet bill and car interior decorated with stains that would be very hard to remove.

Fortunately for him I had already solved his problem. By the time he had finished arguing with himself about what I'm sure were the ethical and pragmatic pros and cons, I had disappeared in the whiteout. As I became only a shadow of my former self, I only hoped the incident would remind him to pound on his car hood and sides before starting the engine any time he left the car out.

To my mind it was his duty to alert any of us squatting under the hood or in the wheel wells to high-tail it out in time. He couldn't expect us to read his mind and respond appropriately, though sometimes humans get very huffy about our not acceding to their expectations. Giving us a head's up would help other animals avoid such massive physical destruction. That way it would leave him with fewer seemingly insolvable, messy problems.

4

SAVING ONESELF

Regarding my foot, I can only guess that the accumulating snow on the ground helped me save what was left of it. It bathed the wide ankle-high gash while the cold kept the bleeding to a minimum. I had already lost a lot of blood. How much I didn't really know but I definitely felt weaker. It made my head bob even more. Licking the wound and trying to keep the foot up out of the dirt and grime wherever I went I'm sure likewise helped. But the dribbling, partial amputation was likely to attract predators.

Having only three good legs and not much available energy further hindered my balance, coordination, agility, and speed. Thus, attempting to avoid vicious feral dogs, cats protecting their territory, hateful humans, or vehicles was going to be an even bigger challenge. I wasn't sure I was up to it. How would I meet my survival demands? I couldn't successfully run, jump, or defend myself. My brain whirled. All I knew was that I had to try whatever I could.

I had never been a fighter even though my mother had taught me the basics of cat martial arts for defense. However, in my present state of disrepair, I was unsure how I could possibly execute any of those skillful maneuvers. Balance and leverage were the key to doing them properly. I was quickly learning that the world is frequently a hard and unfeeling place. That you need to be able to use all the skills you have. And "survival of the fittest" is more than a glib catch-phrase.

Like all young cats, before my near-dismemberment, I couldn't conceive of anything truly terrible ever happening to me. It's a strange thing how youth seems to regard itself as immortal until something startling shakes that faith. For me it was more than witnessing my mother's sudden, violent death. At that time I still felt immune, sure that even though it had happened to her, it couldn't possibly happen to me. Ah, the youthful dichotomy of belief and reality. Thankfully circumstances and age have made me a little wiser. Now I know for sure that this is not the "best of all possible worlds" for cats and I'm not immortal, and likely never was.

Three weeks went by as I hobbled along searching for food and shelter. On several occasions I had to secret myself from neighborhood roaming canines that had picked up my scent. One time I somehow managed to claw my way up an old Siberian elm tree to a low branch where I hid hugging the main trunk's dark, rough bark. Did that make me a "tree hugger"? Yeah, probably. I loved trees. My climbing ability, while questionable for most cats, was, I felt, satisfactory for my needs. However, my strength had been reduced by more than half of its previous level. Another time I managed to squeeze into a narrow, rotting log, just inches out of reach of a slavering, snarling snout.

Chunky adult raccoons likewise challenged me when they too had located a stash of dry cat pellets put out by caring residents for homeless or wandering felines. They stood up on their hind legs, growled, looked at me askance as if chuckling in amazement, and then waddled on all fours after me. Despite their girth, they were fast, though, perhaps, not running as fast as they could after me. After all, why bother? Those encounters were too close for comfort and quickly nearly exhausted my reserves. Each time it was taking me longer to regroup.

No matter what I did, pain in that truncated limb was a constant companion. I suspected it was from nerve damage as well as a raging infection. By now the wound had ballooned my foot and leg to more than twice their normal size. Occasionally, it would gape open and exude a putrid, viscous fluid. As a result of what was an obvious systemic affliction, I was starting to feel continuously fatigued, lethargic, feverish, and weak. Day by day my pace was becoming slower and slower.

Attempting to make my rounds of houses and food establishments where humans recognized me by my unusual gait and sometimes left me tidbits to eat was taking more physical effort than it had in the past. Moreover, if another cat challenged me for the food, I wasn't up to combat for what was clearly mine. Accessing basic nutrition was increasingly an arduous and less successful task.

Furthermore, licking the gash on my foot which had seemed to help initially now seemed to help less and less as time wore on. And, maybe, it was even making the situation worse. I didn't know. I seemed to do it mindlessly out of habit. My thinking was less clear. In my formerly-"normal" state I was always alert and laser-focused in spite of my perpetual motion. Now I seemed to be operating on autopilot most of the time. Constant hunger pangs didn't help my situation any.

As if circumstances couldn't get any worse, my left hip which had begun to manifest a separate, low-level, chronic discomfort after the accident was getting worse. I had thought that I had probably strained some muscles when my foot was caught and shredded. But so much time had elapsed. Shouldn't they have recovered by now if that were all it was? Perhaps, it was something more serious, like a torn ligament or leg bone fracture. I worried that maybe my leg would ultimately rot away from gangrene. Or, instead, maybe I'd die well before that happened from one of too many causes to count. The more tired I became, the more morbid I became.

Since humans in general didn't seem to notice my extra "distress," it was heartwarming that two people did acknowledge it. In fact, they actually appeared to want to assist me. One was a male human. When jogging along Sagebrush Drive, he noticed me. With a look of concern he started to approach me. That was okay because I immediately sensed he wanted to be kind. In my deteriorating state I was ready and willing to accept any kindness tossed my way.

He whipped his cell phone out of his fleece track suit jacket. Good. I hoped he was calling a veterinary kitty ambulance for me. Or maybe he was calling one of the local no-kill animal shelters to pick me up and work their magic. Either one would get me the help I needed right away. I waited with optimistic enthusiasm.

What? Oh, no! Did I hear that right? He was calling "Animal Control?" No, not Animal Control! I'd heard so many horror stories from other cats about animals captured by Animal Control. They were scooped up, dropped off at city pounds, and dumped in a cage to lie on a cold concrete floor. There they'd wait in pain for medical help that would *never* come. I couldn't believe he understood the consequences and implications of doing that. That sounded like state-subsidized cruelty to me.

I didn't really know why he had called them, other than the obvious. But I was not about to stick around to find out if I had misunderstood. No way, no how! Even though my life since my mother's death had been incredibly hard, I felt I'd rather die on my own terms in the snow than in a prison cell of human neglect or abuse worthy of urban legends. Fuzzy-brained but determined, I hobbled away as rapidly as I could.

At another time a female human volunteer from one of the companion animal rescue non-profits saw me on Walden Road. I had seen her before carefully trapping homeless cats so I knew she was compassionate about helping us. That was a good sign. I relaxed a little.

Because I also knew that most—maybe all—of the non-profits in the area provided medical care of some kind, I would have my wound tended to—finally. I breathed a sigh of relief. When she reached for me, I melted into her arms. I'd acquiesce to anything she wanted if her group's veterinarian would heal me.

Carefully picking me up, she examined me from nose to tail, and inspected my left leg at length. Nervous and anxious, I began to shake rapidly. She looked questioningly at me. No doubt she thought my tremors were associated with my infected limb. Grimacing, she pulled out her cell phone.

I was in my head. I toyed with visions of being ensconced on a dry, warm kitty bed with delectable food available and IV tubes feeding me liberating medication. She was talking excitedly to someone, saying things I didn't completely understand. I ignored most of what she said. I had planning to do.

But out of the morass of babble, one word pricked up my ears. Even in my dull-witted, feverish state, I recognized the word "amputate." What? Wait a minute! What are you saying? You're not suggesting I have my leg hacked off, are you? Is someone on the other end of the call suggesting it? I panicked. No way, kiddo!

What in the world was she thinking? As my anxiety swelled, I called to her, Hey! How about a professional medical opinion? You're not a vet! I know there must be treatment *options*. Was that her intention? That shivered my timbers in ways I would soon not forget.

I pictured myself without that limb. I was ambulating with only a modicum of speed when I had four (semi-)functional limbs. No, I couldn't allow that. Amputation was the very last resort, like woodpiles. I liked my left leg, or—well—what remained of it. In fact, I was very fond of it because it had always been an amiable part of me.

Nope! Sick or not, I wasn't about to simply relinquish it because a rescue volunteer thought it had to go. With that motivating me, I struggled out of her arms, landing on my right side in the snow. As she fumbled for her cell phone which fell as well, I limped away.

Serendipitously, there was a 1966 Airstream Overlander trailer parked in a snowy yard nearby. I hid under the rear of it. It saddened me that once again I felt I had to escape from a human who was ostensibly trying to help me. But Animal Control or amputation: Those were my disheartening choices, especially with so few humans willing to help around. As my thinking became more befuddled, I saw my problem as: There was help and then there was *help*. And I was particular about which one I would accept.

Once away from the human, I decompressed a little. Everything felt futile. I didn't feel capable of making these life and death determinations as my pain and infection expanded exponentially. Was I still *compos mentis*? I was beginning to doubt it. Above all, I wanted my mother to comfort me ... to make the right decisions for me ... to make it all better. Sadly, at some level I really knew my mother could no longer intervene on my behalf. I felt like lying down in the snow and blubbering like a human baby.

5

FINDING A FRIEND IN NEED

Under the Airstream, I came face to face with what was at one time a large black dog. It was chained to an open, make-shift dog house a few feet away. The wind was swirling in vortices at its entrance. Ice frosted the wooden floor as small chunks formed nodules on the threadbare remnant of some once-upon-a-time fuzzy bathroom rug. Originally the rug apparently had been arranged to partially cover the openings between the floors wood planks. Two dirt-caked steel dishes sat nearby. While the assigned food dish was empty, the water dish contained only a crystalline glaze of brown.

The shade of a former-dog which was curled upon itself on a four-by-five-foot piece of appliance shipping cardboard was shivering rapidly. On my closer inspection it no longer looked black or young. White hairs randomly covered its sore-camouflaged body. Its muzzle was almost totally silver. Bones protruded from its body at odd angles like masticated Buffalo Wings scattered in the trash.

When I first recognized I was not alone, I froze— well, as much as I could control. A dog! All my frightening encounters with canines rushed to mind. On the spot I had to decide: What is the situation? What should I do? Escaping back into the arms of the animal rescuer didn't appeal at all. As I tried to unscramble my thoughts, I kept the dog in my peripheral vision.

During my seconds of indecision, the old dog lifted its heavy, skin-stretched head. When it moved its jowls, it seemed to form a welcoming smile. Something in its rheumy eyes told me it was very glad for company. There was a small attempt at a gentle woof. But without any energy behind it, it sounded more like heavy, chronically-obstructed breathing.

The dog moved its spindly legs listlessly from a fetal to a more open position, nodding its head. At first I wasn't sure it was nodding at me or merely had the same neurological tremor I had with my head. Since it had no other involuntary movements, I took this to be an invitation to lie against its belly so we could share body heat. This was an invitation I could not refuse. This situation was funny in an absurd way. I was being given shelter in a literal and figurative storm from someone who was not much better off than I was.

As I lay against the much-used nipples and sharp skin-covered ribs, I knew this dog must have had an even worse life than I had had. At least I was young and free. I couldn't imagine anything worse than being chained in one place season after season, year after year, being no more recognized than an old chunk of concrete, unloved and unattended to, simply neglected.

The dog pulled her legs up and around me, resuming her fetal position. Slowly, tenderly, she began to lick my head and belly, as she had no doubt done to her many litters of puppies. Purring in response, I saw that she quickly dropped off again, snoring loudly even as she continued to shiver.

Much of the night as I cuddled close to the old dog, I dreamt about my mother. I was wrapped in her loving paws as before. She nuzzled and groomed me. Everything was right with the world. I felt secure, protected, and cared for. Then the scene abruptly switched to Loma Larga where *I* was holding her close, protecting her as she finally departed this earthly realm. The gnawing pain of her leaving was once again boring into my stomach wall. I clutched the mother dog more tightly as I reached out to my own mother. If I could have shed a tear as the temperature continued to drop, I would have.

When morning approached, it did so in hazy increments. I awoke before the sun was up but was still caught up in my dream-like state. I didn't want to let go of it. The emotional memory of my mother dying hung over me like a lead shroud, weighing me down. I badly wanted to go back to where she and I were still together as a family, enjoying each other's company in the sunshine. Maybe if I lay really still I could slip back to that part of the dream. But closing my eyes and snuggling closer to the mama dog didn't work. Once I was on the verge of wakefulness, there was no going back. Still, I lay there a while longer, seeing and feeling her, pretending we were one again.

But now hunger pangs competed with my grief. Trying not to move too much so as not to disturb mama dog, I glanced over at the food dish for a sign of anything edible. The bowl was still empty. I licked my paws, stretching my toes apart to clean every crevice, wondering where I could get a meal. Maybe someone would remember this particular morning to put out some kibble or canned food for mama dog. Maybe I should wait a little longer just in case.

Mama dog had really helped keep me warm the night before. To thank her I bunted her with my head and rubbed my small body against hers. I continued to rub against her abdomen and chest until I noticed something odd. I couldn't see or feel her chest rise and fall now. In fact, there appeared to be no movement in her body whatsoever. I tried to push myself under her front limbs again but they seemed to be locked in place. No matter how hard I tried their rigidity was greater than my strength. With my ear against her chest, I heard she was no longer wheezing. For a moment I was glad for her until I realized, likewise, she was no longer breathing, just like my mother.

My heart sank. For a moment I felt as though I'd swallowed an apple. I was both saddened and dumbfounded. In her last hours this sweet creature had reached out to me, a perfect stranger. I wasn't even a dog, much less a "normal" cat! She had comforted me and warmed me. She had kept me alive for another day. But, in the meantime, she had passed away.

Now I found I was caught on the horns of guilt and gratitude. Did I really deserve this gift? Mama dog must have thought so or she wouldn't have done it. And maybe in exchange for her generosity I may have made her last hours warmer, more physically intimate, and emotionally satisfying. I truly hoped so.

At this moment I wished the human stories about the so-called "Rainbow Bridge" were true in some way, shape, or form. I wanted this kind dog to finally find some peace and happiness. In my fantasy Rainbow Bridge I pictured her there energized, fully renewed, joyfully romping on the grass in the sunshine, free, and never concerned again about not having enough food and water or a safe, comfortable place to sleep.

Yes, Over the Rainbow Bridge she would be regaled with loving attention and would luxuriate in every minute of it. It was a nice image. I wondered why the world wasn't more like that for animals. Sighing, I thought that at least she and my mother were beyond pain now. If only I could be sure my being with the old mama dog had given her exhausted heart a temporary incandescent glow. I gave her several heartfelt farewell licks on her stiff jowl before I wistfully departed.

As I slipped out from under the Airstream, I felt the need to express my increasing rage about how obviously bereft mama dog's life had been and what a lousy death she had suffered. There was no excuse for such inhuman cruelty. I wanted to believe humans were basically good but sometimes their barbaric, destructive behavior was beyond my comprehension. How could some people be so kind, thoughtful, and selfless while some others could be so sadistic, thoughtless, and narcissistic? I wanted to do something to protest mama dog's pain-wracked, untimely, and so unnecessary death.

So I did the only thing I was equipped to do. Walking up the front step to the adobe house door, I turned around, raised my tail, and let loose with a night's full bladder spray of urine. It took several seconds to unload. Then I attempted to jump up to hit the low doorbell with my right paw. Of course I could only graze it. Somehow they *had* to hear me.

I slapped at the front door with my right paw, resulting in a muffled rap. My adrenaline was now surging. Gathering all my strength and coordination, I threw my front paws onto the rustic wood several times, screeching my loudest. Hear me! Dammit! Hear me!

Silently I begged someone would hear it and come out. I wanted them to find mama dog. I willed them to care, though that was highly unlikely after all they had made her endure. I willed them to treat her body respectfully, to gently wrap her in a blanket, find a peaceful resting place, and bury her with the honor she deserved. In my reverie I hoped at a minimum they wouldn't leave her corpse to be fodder for the starving coyotes that were incautiously traveling into populated areas seeking any remnant as a meal.

But mostly what I wanted was for them to behold the result of my unbridled anger. Yellow vertical lines decorated the weathered door, seeping into cracks which I hoped would reek of cat piss in the summer heat. The droplets formed amber icicles at the lower edge, frosting the sill like motor oil. Because I believe in doing things right, I had made sure the Welcome mat was appropriately drenched and crystalizing.

My only regret was that I didn't have a bowel movement ready to place in the center of the mat to be stepped on. Of course, if I had had opposable thumbs, a paper bag, matches, and my solid waste, I could have done what mischievous children have done for decades. I could have packaged and set that lovely little gift ablaze, guaranteeing someone would stomp on it with a "Help! Fire!" You miserable excuses for the label "human"!

But, ooh! What a delightfully squishy surprise! Ah, yes. *That* would have been the *pièce de résistance*.

6

TRYING TO KEEP GOING

Two weeks went by so slowly. I no longer had an accurate sense of time. Days melded together. Mama dog and my mother occasionally flitted through my mind with sweet sadness. Sometimes they blended together in one deep universal sigh. I was barely slogging along. It was clear now that if approached by a predator, running and escaping would require more strength and agility than I could possibly muster.

Finding anything to eat was quickly getting to be beyond my ken. More times than I wanted to contemplate I had taken to eating snow and chewing on frozen twigs, leaves, and bark. Not all that digestible in the first place, the plant material was quickly regurgitated, leaving me feeling even worse.

Early one evening the small waves of snow were reflecting the moon's rays in a thousand mirrors illuminating the landscape with Halogen intensity. It was like daylight as I clumsily limped through a slightly rundown neighborhood. Yards were weed-strewn, with seed heads and desiccated stems poking through the white blanket, like triggers for buried IEDs. The homes here were replete with cracking, chipping, stained stucco.

My destination was a wooden shed which sat beside a one-story old adobe house off Corrales Road on the Rio Grande side. The silver-weathered door was slightly ajar. Its black wrought-iron latch hung askew. I optimistically thought I'd give it a try—that is, *if* I could make it. It wouldn't be that warm but perhaps it would be enough to prevent hypothermia. How warm would that be? How cold was I already? I was no longer aware of my increased shivering and benumbed paws.

If I were lucky, I mused, I would be the only one in there. Wait. No, that wasn't realistic. Many others would be seeking the same life-saving shelter. But, then again, that could be fine too—maybe even better if they were companionable. Yeah, sure, more bodies could generate and share more heat. That was the way to go.

Suddenly I pictured a cheery room full of genial cats. They were grooming one another and welcoming me to enter. Some would be lighting up their catnip reefers while others would be tossing balls of yarn or joking with resident mice. They all would be passing the sardine can to me, begging me to join the festive gathering. Not just a refuge but party time! My dreamy mind basked in that glowing vision.

Slipping and sliding, my shambling gait inched me across the mirrored surface of the narrow two-lane road until I lost my balance. Suddenly my feet flew out from under me. I fell ... hard. My body skidded toward the snow removal-packed wall at the side of the road. In keeping with Murphy's Law, which I've heard humans in passing joke about, I landed on my left hip—my feline equivalent of bread's buttered side down. I lay there, engulfed in pain, made worse by my constant tremors. My brain felt full of cotton wool. And my febrile skin was on the brink of frostbite despite my heavy coat.

Gasping for breath, struggling for all I was worth, I was still unable to right myself. If only the multitude of cats entertaining themselves inside the shed could help me twist my body around. If they could do it just enough to place three paws on the road surface under me ... No, better still, if they could hoist me onto their shoulders or place me on a large velvet pillow and carry me inside.

I'm not sure but I think I called to them. However, for some reason they didn't answer. My expectation was that once they were alerted to my pressing need for assistance, they would rush outside to help me. Hey, guys, I'm here! Where are you? Baffled by their lack of response, I called as loudly as I could. It sounded more like a mouse squeak. I'm here. Why aren't you helping me?

I could feel my heart squeeze with icy trepidation. I tried to make light of the situation. Maybe they were too zoned out on *Nepeta cataria* to hear me. As I tried to call out to them again, no sound came out of my mouth. Everything was growing dimmer. Blackness was reducing my vision to a pinhole which then disappeared. I passed out.

When I partially awoke, my lower back and hip socket were screaming at me. The cacophony rang deafeningly in my ears. I'm sure I meowed my loudest, asking anyone—*anyone*—within hearing distance to help me. I'm sure I promised my fellow felines they could go back to their buttermilk and tuna when they finished with me. There was still no response. I passed out again.

As I re-opened my eyes, I saw the specter of dozens of cats crowded around me. Talking amongst themselves, they looked concerned and distraught. I tried to reach out a front paw to them, to beckon them closer to hear me. But they disappeared like blue flames in a stiff breeze.

The cold was seeping into my marrow, stiffening my limbs, reducing my tremors. I felt sleepier than I had ever felt before. The strong pull of letting go to drift off was hard to resist. It didn't seem to be something to fear. It didn't seem all that bad after everything I had already experienced. It was so easy. All I had to do was just close my eyes and give myself up to it. I would finally be done with the pain and struggle. It sweetly beckoned to me. I was ready to follow.

Suddenly the image of my mother flashed before me. Looking sad and disappointed, she whispered, "You simply can't accept this as the end. You have to do what you can to hang on. You must fight. You must survive. I'm sending you all my strength." At the same time, mama dog appeared, holding open her paws to me, saying, "I'm here for you. I'll help you. It's okay. It's easy. No more pain and struggle. Just let go."

Staring into the frigid, dark sky, part of me resonated to my mother's pleas. I beseeched the

Universe, Please don't let me die here like my mother and mama dog. Give me a second chance. Let someone, anyone discover, care, and save me. I'll do whatever I have to do to make me worthy.

As I lay there, stunned, fighting unconsciousness for what seemed like days, a cadaverous coyote trotted by. What undoubtedly was once beautiful coat was now shabby red, gray, and black matted tufts. It came toward me, sniffing as if it couldn't believe that Fate had actually led it to some much-needed sustenance. As it was about to pick up my body in its white jaws, a car approached slowly.

The speed limit was only 25 mph on that winding stretch of Corrales Road but the road was slick. The headlights swept the street ahead of it, as if searching. Abandoning its meal, the disappointed coyote quickly turned tail and loped off. It knew full well that avoiding humans enhanced the probability of its survival, in spite of its hunger. Droplets of its saliva lingered on my fur, turning crystalline, like frozen tears.

Because of my increasing hypothermia, I felt myself welcoming my delirium. It made everything surreal. The coyote had seemed only a phantasm. The vehicle's headlights were a will-o'-the-wisp, a ghost-like phenomenon that was trying to lead me off the path of my destiny. Pain was nearly a thing of the past.

Detached from emotion, I had a transient minute of lucidity. Calmly I wondered if the car would skid in my direction, hit me, and perhaps even kill me. Would it matter since I was already easing myself off this plane of existence? It was action happening on a movie screen. I could only watch and abstractly conjecture as I floated above the scene.

As my mother's words echoed, my soporific brain teetered momentarily back into consciousness so I could focus on the car. What if, I considered, the driver spotted me? What if this human did something to help, instead of doing nothing at all ... or merely driving on? At this hour on a weeknight the traffic was light here. There was no telling when another vehicle might come by ... and possibly see me frozen to that spot. What if?

Before my accident, whenever I could, I tended to avoid humans unless I could sense their positive feelings toward me. When I did feel those warm, embracing vibes, I might warily approach them or let them approach me. First wide-eyed then squinting at them, I would perk up my ears and raise my tail like a wavering flagpole of invitation. Nine times out of ten my vibes were right about them and they showed affection, giving me a pet or something to nibble.

In my current situation, I was in no position to do any of that irrespective of whether my antennae picked up positive or negative energy. I was not only figuratively stuck but also starting to literally stick, unable to respond in any meaningful way, friendly or otherwise. Concentrating was hard because the cold's pull was too tantalizing. It kept drawing me back into my twilight state where I glided among the celestial orbs and diaphanous visions of my mother.

As I lay there, I tried to watch and listen but my attention was dwindling. I was too physically encumbered to discern any human emotions or catch any empathetic thoughts. However, I *could* see the person had stopped well in advance of hitting me. I guessed that was encouraging but I wasn't sure it really mattered any longer. As I grew sleepier, I was grasping less at my mother's optimistic straws of survival.

With the headlights still on me and the turn signal clicking, a female human emerged from the driver's side. She made her way slowly to where I lay. Was she really "human"? Or was she a supernatural being—an "angel"—what religious humans talked about as a protector and guide? Headlights shining from behind her glowed around her like a halo. Wasn't that how some people spoke about angels? Cats don't have angels so I didn't know.

Before I dropped off again, slowly letting myself go, my mother's encouraging voice squeezed through the miasma. "NO! Don't let go!" she whispered again. "You don't have to *do* anything to be 'worthy' of a second chance. Just being you and alive is more than deserving enough." Her words reverberated in the stillness with comfort and love.

With what seemed like my last ounce of energy, my mother and I screamed together silently at the human, hoping she might be able to hear me. Help! Please help me! Please!

7

TRUSTING WHEN YOU'RE AFRAID

Kneeling on both knees on the ice, the female human gently pressed her ear to my chest to see if I were still breathing. Paralyzed, my breathing which had been heavy and labored only seconds before now seemed almost to have ceased altogether. I roused only slightly, reflexively to her warm touch. As I had sickened from my infection, my heart rate had increased. But now as my body grew colder, my heart rate slowed and seemed to me barely audible. I wasn't sure she could detect it. With my resolve now buoyed by my mother's urgency, I silently shouted over and over, I'm alive! I'm alive! Help me! Please!

As if she had heard me, the human whispered, "I'm going to help you. But first I have to see what the problems are and how I can safely move you. I'll be careful and try not to hurt you."

Tenderly her fingers moved all over my body, feeling to see if anything, like my back, were broken. It wasn't. Despite my left leg being under my body, the slashed appendage and infection were obvious to her. My hip injury was still hidden. I didn't know what exactly she had determined to do because her thoughts were now coming at me like lazy static.

Humans could be hard to decipher at the best of times. They, unlike cats, were not always particularly logical in their thought processes. Of course, my condition precluded my comprehension of very much except for the most obvious.

Almost immediately she had pulled an old, wool, green, black, and white plaid car blanket out of the backseat and carefully bundled me in it. As she held me against her chest, she gave my body and three legs a very gentle rub down. I assumed it was to get my circulation going while not damaging any frostbitten tissue. She assiduously avoided my left leg.

Contemplation of what had been my imminent demise struggled with thankfulness that perhaps I would not die like my mother or mama dog after all. I was torn. As I muddled my way through which option was best for me, I felt my rescuer lower me onto the passenger seat.

With the heater blowing warm air on me, I temporarily succumbed to the darkness that was beckoning me. She drove off with me to some unknown location. Where didn't matter to me. My body and mind were bobbing serenely in a morphine-like sea.

When I attempted to rouse myself again, I beheld a strange sort of kitty heaven. It was not what I'd expected "Over the Rainbow Bridge" meant. I was in a warm, humid, bright location that smelled fresh. There was no grass, flowers, trees, breeze, sunshine, or other cats playing. Instead clothes were folded on top of a large, white metal box. There was a white cotton line stretched across the end of the light yellow room with some kind of colorful garments hanging from it with small wooden clips.

My rescuer was doing something that as yet made no sense to me. She was lifting my left leg a few degrees in order to place my foot and ankle in a tilted, deep metal bowl which was filled with warm salty water. For a moment I wondered if I was at the seaside. No, that made no sense. My mother had spoken of the existence of the seaside but I had never experienced it.

As I awakened more, it finally seeped through my bacteria-addled cerebrum what was going on. My rescuer was trying to soak my jerky swollen left foot. Unfortunately the awkward maneuver exacerbated my hip pain. I yelped and growled. But I realized she had no way of knowing about my hip. She was simply trying to help my injury. I wanted to be understanding, but the pain—

At that moment I remembered something my mother had passed on to me. It's so odd the things you remember. She said, "Through trial and suffering, you are strengthened in mind, body, and spirit. You are inspired to challenge the impossible, do what's required, and achieve your successes." Okay, if this was necessary for making everything better, I would cooperate as best I could. But there *must* be a better way of doing it.

In spite of the additional discomfort, I was grateful for what I surmised was my Second Chance. Thanks, Mom. I couldn't have done it without you. Determined to show my gratitude, I tried to keep my yelps, growls, and hisses to a minimum. I could tell my rescuer felt guilty about my pain. Every time she dipped my foot she wrinkled her brow, pressed her lips together, and gently stroked my head.

When she finished, she carefully lifted me off the towel and lowered me onto the folded blanket she had wrapped me in which she had already placed on the floor. Next she stationed a three-inch-sided, filled cardboard litter pan about three feet from me. Ah, she had had cats. That was a good sign. I needed reassurance. Beside me she put a bowl of fresh water, one of chicken broth, and one of dry cat food.

Giving me a friendly scratch between my shoulder blades, she surprisingly kissed the top of my bobbing head. I didn't know quite what to make of the behavior. Then she switched on a seven-watt night light and turned off the overhead fluorescent tube. As she was about to the close the door on me, she said, "Goodnight. If you need anything just call me. Don't worry. Tomorrow you'll start getting on the mend."

My night was relatively-speaking more comfortable than most—at least it was inside and warm—but still fraught with pain every time I intentionally, or unintentionally, shifted my body even slightly. With both my foot and hip so unhappy, it was difficult getting into any reasonable sleeping position.

In the morning as she opened what turned out to be the utility room door, she cheerily greeted me, "How are you feeling? Any better?" Such cheeriness was a little hard to take given the circumstances. Then she added, "I know you must be in a lot of pain so I'm sorry I have to move you again. We're going to the vet to see what we can do about your leg."

I mentally groaned. I wanted to say, I know I need medical attention. But, do we have to go someplace? I don't want to be moved. Is it asking too much to have the vet come here?

My reservations were not expressed. Before I could state my feelings, I managed to twist my left hip. Skyrockets took off. Once again I slipped into unconsciousness.

8

MAKING MY WAY BACK?

When I had awakened again only minutes later, I felt my brain was wading in quicksand. I wasn't sure how much time had passed. The last thing I remembered was something about going in her car to get medical help. Were we at the vet already? I looked around. The cobwebs were beginning to clear. No, we hadn't left yet. Oh, crap!

The stricken look on my face must have resonated with her. She reiterated, "I know you're in pain and don't want to move. But it's necessary. You're going to be feeling so much better soon." I thought, Yeah, sure. Too bad the trip couldn't have occurred while I was still unconscious.

Even though she sounded confident and experienced, I didn't feel all that comforted. To prepare myself for what I assumed was to be a jaw-clenching, body-jangling trip I tried to relax as much as I could. But when she lifted my body horizontally, my surging black-panther adrenaline prompted me to tear her arm off. Gritting my teeth instead, I let out a scream that rolled out of the deepest reaches of my viscera.

She then placed me in an extra-large carrier on a thick beige bath towel on my right side. Fortunately it opened at the top as well as at the end. I couldn't imagine being stuffed in through the opening at the end. That type of entry and exit didn't seem all that thoughtful or well-planned out. The carrier gave her plenty of room in which to maneuver me. That also allowed me, once I recovered my composure, to shift my position as needed in the given space when possible and necessary.

My hyperventilation was easing off until she closed the metallic mesh door on the top. Oh, no! I immediately felt trapped. I tried to think positively. The more I fretted and became anxious the more my foot and hip seemed to hurt. My whole body was tensing. Too bad there wasn't yoga for cats. I really could have used some careful stretching and meditative breathing exercises to help me vege out.

The ride to the vet was, as expected, a literal pain in the butt. I thought I would die from it but I obviously didn't. At the Sunrise Veterinary Clinic on Rio Rancho Drive a tall, slim man with gold-rimmed glasses and wearing a white jacket placed me on a cold, metal table on my right side. He examined my entire body. I could tell he and my rescuer knew each other by the way they hugged and casually chatted. I must not have been the first cat she had brought to him. That was reinforced by their temporarily naming me "New Cat" for their medical records.

As they conversed intermittently, he looked in my mouth and ears, palpated my left leg and hip and abdomen, listened to my heart, and checked my lungs. Suddenly, without a word of warning to me, he introduced a foreign object into my rectum. Abruptly wide awake now, I was aghast. No one even asked if it would be okay with me—which it most certainly was not. I was appalled at such an invasion of my privacy but only clenched my teeth and grunted my displeasure. There were bigger issues at hand.

My temperature was elevated, over one hundred and four degrees. Undoubtedly it was due to my foot infection and dehydration. He shaved a small patch of fur off my throat and finally managed to stick a needle into the skin of my weaving neck. While it pinched, it didn't stress me unduly. However, the strong smell of alcohol he'd rubbed on the puncture site turned my stomach.

What further added to my tension was being held tightly by both the vet and a technician as they stuck a large needle under the skin and taped it in place on my right front leg to let fluid flow into my body from a clear plastic bag above me. I looked at them as if to ask, Is that *really* necessary? Besides, you dummies, that's putting pressure on my left hip. I beseeched my rescuer to intervene and asked, Where is that *help* you promised? *When* is it going to occur?

The vet, Dr. George Abernathy, confirmed that my foot and leg were likely infected by what sounded like some Latin gobble-gobble which had caused my pyodema, my infection? When he had me lying stationary on a cold glass plate, he took a whirring picture of my whole left leg. The x-ray revealed a fracture at the top of my left femur where it meets the hip socket. It was starting to heal but was slightly misaligned. He stated it would likely cause arthritic problems as I aged and possibly further interfere with my ambulation. "You know," he said to my rescuer, "he has CHP (cerebellar hypoplasia)." That didn't mean anything to me but she nodded and shrugged.

The way he described the difficulty of re-breaking and resetting the bone sounded as if it was not a useful thing to do for me because of the break location. He added that trying to put in a metal plate or pins likewise would not be constructive due to both the type of break and location. So what did that mean? There wasn't anything he could do about my hip? I hoped he meant other than providing pain medication. In the meantime, I needed a blood transfusion to address my blood loss, anemia, and shock.

The disposition of my foot was another issue. The fan belt had jaggedly torn toes, claws, and pads off. It needed surgery, but not until that bacterial scourge had been eradicated. Dr. Abernathy recommended some antibiotic I had to take orally. I soon would discover that it tasted grotesque. I'd foam at the mouth and drool down my chin and onto my chest. How gross and uncouth!

Consequently, every time my rescuer attempted to introduce the medication syringe into my mouth, morning and night, I fought the object as if it were a rattlesnake attacking me. Still, in the end, I did take it—all of it—with her *firm coaxing*. That is a euphemism for her sneakily opening my jaw, slipping the liquid into my cheek pouch, and repeatedly rubbing my throat downward until I swallowed it. Ugh.

However, despite my attempts to battle her maneuvers, I noted I was beginning to feel the tiniest bit better as the days went on. Even though she was doing all she could to help, still in all, I thought that aspect of my treatment truly sucked.

9

COMMUNICATING WITH HUMANS

My rescuer had to continue to soak my left foot four times a day with warm, salty water. For her to be more successful at it the vet had recommended she use a heavy plastic bag filled with the soaking solution so she didn't have to elevate my leg to accomplish her goal. Thank you, Dr. Abernathy. That suggestion helped a lot. When the leg wasn't raised, the warm water was more comforting to my foot. Moreover, that method prevented my leg movements from sloshing the water all over the place. I even grew to ignore the stinging of the salt.

Even though I still felt under the weather physically, I didn't mind being pampered. In fact, I was starting to believe I might actually survive and recover to the point where I could enjoy such attention. I had no idea if that would truly occur or what would happen after that. If only my mother had had that chance. I knew I felt less close to death, or as my mother referred poetically to it, "shuffling off this mortal coil."

As the medication machine-gunned the offending bacterial invader, my infection waned. I became conscious that I didn't mind staying in my rescuer's house. It wasn't half bad. Okay, in fact, I guess I liked it. It didn't present me with all the exploration and discovery—the sights, sounds, and smells—that being outdoors did. But, then again, it didn't have all the unnecessary excitement of cats, dogs, and teenagers chasing tortoise-like, three-legged me.

I could do without having to fend off claws, teeth, rocks, bb pellets, and Firestone radials. And there was a lot to be said for not struggling in the cold and wet to search out any scrap of food or shelter to keep me alive another hour—or another day.

Until this moment, my rescuer had not called me by any name. I had been too oblivious to really notice or be concerned. Since she was a cat person, I suspected she had waited until I began to recuperate. Now, if my expectations were met, she would provide me with possible names from which *I* could choose. Like most cats, I wasn't interested in her pulling just any name out of the blue and *assigning* it to me. There was cat etiquette about informed consent to consider. Fortunately she seemed to accept this. But when she did offer a list, I was not thrilled, not in the least. "Underwhelmed" is more like it.

Nothing she mentioned quite fit my sense of myself, my multi-faceted personality. For example, I definitely wasn't a "Bob," "Bill," "Sooty," "Fluffy," "Sherman," "Blackie," "Pooky," "Maxie," "Schroedinger," "Pyewacket," "Sushi," "Sam," "Doogie," "Buster," "Cramer," "Scrumptious," or "Cat-Astrophe." "Scrumptious?" That was a little too saccharine for my taste. I wasn't something edible. But that last one?! I hoped it was a joke. It was particularly beneath my dignity. Humans were always trying to be clever with naming cats. Cleverness should have no part in it. Naming should always be a serious, respectful task. The name should reflect a cat's character. Humans can be slow learners.

It's funny how things can just happen, though. She was preparing something for her dinner when I hopped to the stove to paw her leg for attention. When I didn't receive it immediately, I tried leaping, grabbing hold of her jeans pant leg to scale the heights. She looked down at me, a little surprised. Then she grinned broadly, "It never ceases to amaze me how intrepid you are."

"Intrepid"? Was that a name? Hmmm. I thought about it for a minute, rolling it around in the inner recesses of my mind. You know, that's a bit of all right. I could see myself as fearless, undaunted, unflinching, spirited, and indomitable. Yes, I think that's just about right on target! I'm not just a sweet little, cuddly cat. I'm also bold, dynamic, and maybe even a little daring. I lifted my head, squinted at her, wrinkled my nose elevating my whiskers, and then emitted a small chirping sound.

"Yes," she responded with a throaty chuckle, "you're right. 'Intrepid' is very fitting. Glad you thought of it. That calls for a chicken-flavored kitty treat to celebrate your new name." From that moment on I was "Intrepid," a name I religiously answered to whenever she called or spoke to me. I could feel myself proudly living up to my new name.

Now that my rescuer and I were establishing a close bond, I felt more comfortable expressing myself to her. I spoke with thoughts, ear-, eye-, tail-, body-, limb-, and whisker movement. Amazingly she listened and responded. If I wasn't sure of her words all the time, I was sure of her tone and body language and the thrust of her thoughts. Hopefully she could discern what I intended to communicate from my other movement.

Outside the utility room, which continued to be my home base, I'd hobble to her, look at her longingly, lower my eyelids, and lift my whiskers to suggest snuggling. Almost no matter what she was doing at that moment, she would gather me into her arms or onto her lap. I'd writhe and purr, rubbing my face on hers, licking her cheek, or bunting her chest. She would smile and stroke me.

Through trial and error—a process that described everything I did, I helped her discover all my special places I wanted to be scratched. When she scratch-attacked them, I'd get all squinty-eyed, raise my quivering tail, and begin to flick my tongue demonically at nothing in particular. She always laughed at my performance but I never felt insulted. Rewarded for her experimentation, she never left me wanting for touch. It was wonderful. Touch must be the universal bonding behavior for all animals, including humans. Life without it would be desolate, unthinkable, and intolerable.

Unfortunately, despite these happy, tranquil moments, I was soon going to have to experience more excruciating pedal pain. From my perspective, I hadn't been properly made aware that it was now time for what turned out to be the *first* surgery on my foot. I'd have to speak to her about cat-human etiquette and the proscribed alerting me to such things in a timely manner.

10

GOING TO THE VET AGAIN?

Suddenly one evening I didn't receive my nighttime snack. I was shocked. As I thought back on what preceded this, I recalled my curiosity about why my rescuer had taken up my food at six o'clock, leaving me only water. That was strange by itself ... and now this. This series of events distressed me terribly. What did it mean? Like most cats, I don't like change. Change is stressful and anxiety-provoking. I had to let her know this was unacceptable.

But how? What if I didn't climb my kitty stairs to get on her bed with her to snuggle as we always did? If I didn't, she'd know I wasn't happy. That could work. But was that the best way to make my point? Maybe it would be better to get on her bed and not snuggle. I could also remind her vocally and physically—a few well-placed pats with a paw—of what she had "forgotten."

I liked that better. It was a proactive, more direct solution. Cats don't like to beat around the bush when something is amiss. But since we don't speak English and humans don't speak Feline (though I don't know why if they can learn Russian, Chinese, or Urdu), we have to do the best we can with what communications' abilities we have.

As a result of my plan, neither of us got much sleep that night. Moreover, despite my pointing out the error of her ways, she still didn't get up to correct it and feed me. Even worse—and I could barely believe this—she compounded the error the following morning when she didn't offer me my breakfast either. Not even a morsel of chicken paté, a slurp of milk, or a single dry food pellet. And no hint of an apology! When I considered all the energy I had just expended in my nocturnal efforts—well, this was very disappointing.

So what did this mean? Had I misjudged my human? Had she suddenly lost her memory? Was she finally revealing her true self as thoughtless? No, I didn't believe that. That didn't match all she had already done so far. But I didn't understand. All I could think was poor, poor me: starving again. Hadn't I been through enough already? What's next? Back on the streets with all my kitty possessions rolled up in a bandana, tied to a stick I had flung over my shoulder? Dumpster diving? Fending off lions, tigers, and bears, oh, my, with my shredded back leg?

If that wasn't frightening enough, when the cat carrier appeared, my blood pressure shot up. I knew what that meant: a trip to Dr. Abernathy. No, sorry, I had no intention of getting in that torture box again. While I'm sure Dr. Abernathy was nice, he would do more "things" to me that would invariably cause even more pain. So I shuffled to her bedroom and haltingly slithered under my rescuer's platform bed. I figured she would have more difficulty reaching me there than would be worth her effort. Talk about feline optimism.

She was not to be dissuaded. Grunting, she pushed the mattress, which was still covered in sheets and blankets, off the slats that held it up off the floor. Then she shoved the slats aside and unceremoniously scooped me up ... again. After having been deposited into the carrier like a sack of potatoes, I was super-miffed at her. Furthermore, I was royally miffed at myself for having allowed it to happen. As a result, I stayed scrunched down in the carrier, my ears flattened, accompanied by an ongoing low-level growl. She had to know that friends don't do this to friends.

We were back at the vet shortly after dawn so I didn't have much time to continue to show my annoyance. Almost immediately I was taken to the back area, given a tranquilizer to relax me, and a tube was lowered down my throat to give me gas anesthesia. I saw it coming but didn't actually feel it because I was transported to kitty La-La Land. This appointment was all about debriding the dead and dying tissue of the formerly-abscessed gash on my left foot and ankle then suturing it closed.

While Dr. Abernathy scraped, snipped, and, stitched, I was languidly rocking on a sea of aquamarine in a woven-red-willow-switch cradle, surrounded by chunks of raw salmon on which I could daintily dine. A multitude of mice were stroking and fluffing my silken fur, rubbing catnip oil on my paws. The pain in my foot and hip existed only in some other world. The sun was shining, creating a golden glow all around me. The sky was a dazzling gentian blue with wisps of translucent mare's tails scudding across it. Birds were aloft, singing as an antiphonal choir, serenading me. Life was wonderful.

But when I finally awoke much later in the day, all the wonderful delights of the universe had vanished. I felt groggy and thirsty. I was still exhaling the anesthetic gas. And my foot? Boy or boy did it ever H-U-R-T! It was wrapped in lots of gauze and had a crinkled purple elastic fabric holding it fast in place. An opioid-like patch was likewise attached to my leg. As I lay there, again feeling sorry for myself, I noticed the pain was slowing ebbing.

When my rescuer came to pick me up, she was apologetic. "I am so sorry to have to subject you to that procedure and resulting pain. Your foot wound needed to be closed." She hugged and squeezed me and held out to me a leaf of catnip from the plants that grew in profusion in her window sill garden. What, no catnip oil to smooth my paws? By now, my pain was under control and I was feeling almost chipper.

Well, I thought, maybe it will be okay after all. The morphine substitute had already kicked in. I'm not crazy about having had surgery but if my foot gets better because of this, you, my dear rescuer, will have redeemed yourself.

I grabbed the leaf from her hand with my lips, wrapped my tongue around it, raked it over my front teeth releasing the pungent molecules, and tasted it. Hot dog! It was incredible. I wondered if I'd get really high on the narcotizing catnip together with the Fentanyl pain patch. A psychedelic trip maybe? Mice, more chunks of salmon, please. Whaa-hoo!

11

NOT EXPECTING SURGERIES

Back home after four o'clock that afternoon, she placed me on the kitchen floor and presented me with a bowl of tuna broth. Because I'm extremely charitable, I thought, perhaps, I'd accept her apology. This was not too shabby a treat. Of course, by now I was starving after having missed my late night snack, breakfast, and my regular intermittent daytime noshing. As a result, I just about inhaled the sumptuous liquid. Lapping the last droplet, I indirectly "indicated" that a little more would not be out of line. She responded appropriately. Good human.

Please note, I did not beg her. Cats do not beg. We hint, suggest, advise, propose, imply, remind, recommend, nudge, and point out the benefits to all present of being given more of whatever it is. It is dogs who "beg."

Needing a nap, I tapped her leg until I could lead her to a seat. Once she sat on the living room sofa, she promptly lifted me onto her lap where I curled up, as was my prerogative, and began to snore as my tremors relaxed. Because I had been good about not licking or chewing on my foot before surgery, my rescuer and the vet had decided not to employ an Elizabeth collar to restrict my interfering with the wound dressing. I've seen those collars on homed cats who struggled mightily with them in order to walk, eat, drink, scratch, and eliminate. My not having one was a BIG relief for which I was grateful.

Only occasionally would I touch my sewn-up back left paw with my tongue or mouth. I suspect my rescuer wasn't sure if I did it then because of the still-lurking pain or the annoyance of having my foot bound tightly. The Fentanyl patch had been good for only three-to-four days, so the rest of my healing would be opioid-free. That meant my left hind foot would remain somewhat tender, making touching the ground with it or putting any weight on it a definite no-no.

Six months went by of lounging in my new home. Eating regularly, I also discovered delicacies that I'd rarely been able to scrounge as a homeless cat. I was now sleeping whenever and wherever I chose, no longer worried about being attacked in my sleep.

Where I slept mostly was with my rescuer. At night when she slept on her side, I curled up behind her knees. When she lay on her back, I either draped myself around her head like an *haute couture* chapeau or positioned myself spread-eagle on her chest, nuzzling her throat or licking her chin raw. From my perspective we were quickly becoming like two aspects of one being. I liked that.

And then it happened again! I could *not* believe it. At six o'clock in the evening my food vanished. My late night snack and the following breakfast never appeared. Uh, oh! Been there and done that. The writing was on the Colonial white, random texture of peaks and valleys of the knockdown-finished walls.

Hey! What about that promise you made to apprise me of upcoming events that affected me?

I didn't wait to consider the meaning of life and the universe. I started to run to hide under the bed. She was on my heels as I skirted the kitchen corner, catching me in mid-gallop as I rounded the bedroom door. Drat! Stuffed under her arm like a pair of sweaty gym shorts, I was then unceremoniously hauled into the utility room, dropped into the towel-lined carrier, and packed off to the vet.

When were these excursions into the realm of renewed pain going to stop? Hey, guys, I have gotten used to not using my back left leg. And if I didn't use it, it didn't hurt that much. Can't we just leave it at that? No one was listening. I think she was probably ignoring me.

This time Dr. Abernathy was going to perform a little reconstructive surgery to try to make my back foot more useable. "Try"? I'd have preferred he didn't refer to it as "trying." How about some reassurance? Tell me know you "know" you can do it. Tell me it will be wonderful. Tell me I can participate in the Feline Division of the Boston Marathon!

What he had to do was restructure my foot. Currently the pads and claws that remained had been crowded together in order to close the wound. That had resulted in a lot of pressure, with remaining claws every which way, stabbing my few foot pads.

By this time I had determined that walking on what remained of my foot was something I was never going to do again. That wasn't great but I could live with it. But now the vet planned to remove a toe joint and pad to make the foot as pain-free and functional as possible. Yeah, well, we'll see about that. I admit to having been highly skeptical.

Adding further insult to injury, no one had seen fit to tell me they were also going to do "something else" as well. Yes, they were going to do the unspeakable. I was to be neutered at the same time. Since no one had asked me my druthers, I apparently had no choice in the matter, no informed consent.

That seemed such a shame. My life had been such that I hadn't had much chance—okay, honestly, *no* chance—to share my genetic heritage to keep my line going. And, now they were arbitrarily closing that door permanently for me. There'd be no little "Intrepids" to add to the kitten population.

But, upon long and careful consideration since then, maybe it was just as well. I had seen far too many kittens that were born homeless than could be rescued, much less adopted. So many young lives were snuffed out due to cruelty, injury, or illness. And those who survived too often went on to live hand-to-mouth existences, always one meal, assault, or weather condition away from disaster or Animal Control euthanasia.

When the two surgeries were over, I was thankful for the Fentanyl patch again. This time it benefitted both surgical areas—one which I could shakily lick and one which I couldn't.

12

HAVING WHAT YOU WANT

As I spent many weeks recovering, my rescuer doted on me. By now I no longer thought of her as my rescuer. She was my *Special Friend*. I had made her an honorary member of the Cat species and a designated "Life-Long Companion," albeit a fur-less one (that was a shame but not her fault). Whatever I wanted (except for a cessation of medication or therapy I needed) she provided.

Sometimes I have wondered about humans, their motivations and resulting emotions. For example, did my Special Friend feel guilty about all she had put me through—all the pain, anxiety, and frustration she had helped create? Or was she just glad I was finally alive, healthy, and well on my way to my new life? They didn't seem mutually exclusive to me. So maybe it was a little of the former and a lot of the latter.

From my own experience with my beloved mother and my decision to finally leave her after she died, I knew it was a tough balancing act, at least for cats. Was it the same with humans? Did they struggle with conflicting feelings of compassion and analytical pragmatism? As I watched my Special Friend, I suspected that cats and humans weren't so very different in dealing with these life challenges.

While my Special Friend was always there for me, giving me what I desired and needed, I was certain to return the favor. That is to say I didn't take her attention for granted or take advantage of her generosity. No, indeed. I gave as good as I got. But it was not only because it was the right thing to do. It was also because I really *wanted* to.

It might surprise some humans that cats have a Golden Rule. I suspect that ours was the basis of what humans millennia ago "conjured up" to be their own. It wouldn't be the first time humans have taken credit for something we cats created. The human version may have been developed by the Egyptians who revered us as sacred providers of protection and justice. They even mummified us as they did their royalty. It was too bad, however, they couldn't wait until we died naturally of our own accord in order to do it.

Since cats first appeared on Earth, kittens have been imbued by their elders with the requirement to do unto others as they would have others do unto themselves. It's our highest form of reciprocation. We employ it with humans as well, especially where they express positive regard toward us.

In looking back from my kitten days to my foot reconstruction, I mused over what I had wanted most of all to be my life. Anchored in what my mother had taught me, I had wanted what my mother never had. I had wanted the opportunity to have a loving and protected home—perhaps best achieved by having a human. That meant having one who listened to me and shared with me a mutually-caring relationship. That meant being respected as a cat with my cat behaviors and needs.

I had learned that to fully achieve that, now that I was no longer homeless, I would have to pull my own weight in the daily cat-human transaction. As long as there was reciprocity, patience, and tolerance on both sides, it would all come together. It would work for us both. Fortunately, my Special Friend had likewise already been schooled in these specific transaction requirements so I didn't have to *try* to teach her. As I've noted, teaching humans is like trying to climb down a tree forwards.

While I still longed for the positive stimulation the outdoors held, I found I could, over time, get my Special Friend to take me out on a long leash and harness to experience, more or less, what I wanted. There was less "chasing" of squirrels, lizards, mice, and birds. There was also less stealthily creeping up on dogs who trespassed her property, leaping at them with honed claws at the ready, and scaring the pooh out of them. But I could still explore, attempt to climb trees, and "hunt" (well, my own version of predation).

As for my back left foot, she encouraged me to use it both inside and outside as soon as the surgical scars had healed. I had been resigned even after the last surgery that I would never fully regain the use of it. As a result, it did take me a while to realize that I no longer had to baby my foot or avoid using it.

Not walking on it had become a habit. And some habits are hard to break even when you know they are no longer useful. To my amazement I found I actually could use it! And because the femur fracture also had healed I could walk on that foot without any pain. What a relief! Thank you, Dr. Abernathy. I guess I shouldn't have doubted you.

However, what was left of the foot itself bore little resemblance to a normal foot. After all my surgical and non-surgical procedures, it was kind of pointed and oddly-shaped. There were just two digital toe pads and two claws and most of the metacarpal pad. At first I felt shy about it. It looked somewhat like a pirate's peg leg. It took about a month for me to dismiss my cosmetic concerns. I was having too much fun to be bothered.

This reminded me of a quotation by George Bernard Shaw my mother shared with me once (I have no idea where she heard it) about unnecessarily hanging on to anger or pain or some dysfunctional behavior: "People become attached to their burdens sometimes more than the burdens are attached to them."

With my Special Friend's encouragement, my mother's words of wisdom, and Dr. Abernathy's skills, I became a "four-footed" cat again. However, I would never make the cat Olympics in track and field. My high-jumping onto counters, shelves, furniture, the mantelpiece, and television required more back-feet leverage and a stronger left hip than I could manage. Okay, I admit it. With my CHP I couldn't have done it anyway. Consequently, her foodstuffs, art objects, and entertainment electronics were safe from my play and exploration.

Not being a "normal" domestic cat is in the eye of the beholder. I had never let my differences bother me. They were just differences. All cats had differences. What was important was that I did what I could do and wanted to do. And, above all, I made a point of enjoying discovering myself, what was meaningful to me, and my purpose. Yes, cats do search for meaning and purpose—within their own context, of course—once their basic physiological needs have been met. But, unlike humans, cats just don't talk about it all the time.

In general I found that everything I needed and wanted was already well within my levitational reach. (I was a very fortunate cat after all.) And when it wasn't within my reach, well, I frequently found a way to work around it. Never underestimate the ingenuity of a cat fueled with a goal, purpose, and lots of motivation.

Speaking of purpose and motivation, I had no idea what my Special Friend had in store for me once I was walking again. It would never have occurred to me. But in retrospect, it was the perfect next step.

13

TAKING THE NEXT STEP: SHARING

It started with—oh, no—being put into the cat carrier again. I was less frightened each successive time the carrier appeared, but I couldn't be sure what the consequence would be. However, instead of going to the vet, we went to a hospital. It was a human hospital, not an animal one. Being leery at first, I stayed quietly against the back wall of the carrier until I could get my bearings. I hadn't been prepared for this.

We had begun paying visits to children's hospitals where they allowed "therapy animals." I didn't know what that meant. At first it occurred to me I was going there to get physical therapy. That made no sense whatsoever. I'd been through the rigors of extensive physical therapy. No. I was there for another reason— one that was not focused on me per se.

Apparently my Special Friend had taken courses to be certified in animal-assisted psychotherapy. That meant she and I together would provide some kind of "therapy" to others. Me provide therapy? What a lofty, somewhat nutty idea. I hadn't been trained to do that. Furthermore, I had no idea what it entailed. However, as I mulled it over, I did recall something out of the ordinary that could have been relevant to coming to see children.

Previously a female human had had me take all sorts of behavior, personality, character, and interpersonal communication skills "tests." At the time I didn't think of it as tests exactly. It was more like her doing something to see how I'd respond. It was fun in a way. "Tests" sounds a whole lot more high falutin' than it was. All I had to do was be myself.

Anyway, as a result of my days working with her, they "certified" me as an honest-to-goodness "therapy cat." I don't know if there was more to it than my not hissing, growling, biting, or clawing anybody. But because I am such a sweetheart I let any and all strangers pet and fondle me. If that's being a "therapy cat," what's not to love.

Still, visiting the children was a little scary at first because of all the hospital smells, noisy machines, and people scurrying about. I was there because most of them had some kind of challenge they had to overcome. As I saw it, my challenge had been my sheared off left foot. While others pointed primarily to my lack of coordination, I had always taken that as a given, something part of me, different but not abnormal. Funny, I had *never* thought of myself as a role model for what I did. Like any cat, I just did what I had to do.

Seeing me get around, with my funny back leg and my total-body jerkiness, made them smile. Some drew pictures of me. Some wrote stories and others wrote poems about me. They each wanted to hold me and stroke me. They examined my peg leg and asked questions about my movement: Would I always be like that? Could I still do what I wanted? I could see changes in their faces.

The cat carrier was quickly becoming my friend. When my Special Friend brought it out, I eagerly let her plant me inside it. It wasn't long before each repeat visit seemed warmer, brighter, more intimate and fun than the last. I looked forward to it. After all, who wouldn't want to be the center of attention of those who truly appreciated you?

This attention was even from children who initially stayed on the periphery and watched the goings on. They pretended not to be interested in me. Some would shift their positions uncomfortably. There was one boy in a wheelchair with steel rods framing his left lower leg and steel pins sticking out of his flesh, like spines on an inflated pufferfish. He looked angry most of the time. When my Special Friend asked him if he'd like to pet me, he refused, stating, "Why should I want to pet a stupid cat that can't even walk properly."

But, as I said, even with the more hard core and reluctant, they all eventually came around. It was as if they couldn't help themselves. I saw them attempt to hide their smiles at my antics. Slowly they came closer. They started asking questions. Soon they joined in wanting to hold me. In fact, if my Special Friend would have let them, they would have monopolized my time. The boy in the steel frame held onto me for as long as he could before my Special Friend and I had to leave. These initial outliers particularly were the ones who checked with us to see that we were coming again soon, on-schedule.

I felt like a magnet and they were the iron filings. There is something so attractive, something so special, about the human-animal bond. It was something I had never experienced before except with my Special Friend. It was an interaction that seemed to work inspirational wonders—not just for them but for me too. Not understanding it, I still reveled in it.

I suspected this was more universal than I could imagine. Sharing all that love, all our mutual identification with pain and frustration, rang out loudly. It was something I was participating in, something that apparently needed airing and addressing. Together we did that. Maybe we lightened the burdens of all present. It made me proud I was part of it. As a cat, you can't get much better than that.

14

DISCOVERING WHAT I'VE LEARNED

Over the years I have learned a great deal. I have gathered a lot of feline wisdom. I have a better understanding of humans, how they think, what they feel, and what truly matters to them. It had reinforced my notion that humans are not that different from cats. That is, we both need respect, caring, touch, and warm relationships. That's a truism I would never have guessed early on. And now I have a better sense of how our species are intimately interconnected—perhaps in some spiritual or cosmic scheme, if you will. My work as a "therapy cat" revealed to me how much we need each other.

All in all, despite my often-harrowing experiences on my journey from being a homeless kitten to a homed cat, I also discovered that I have considerable to be grateful for in spite of my many mistakes. "Gratitude" is a concept unknown to cats as such, although we show it behaviorally all the time with purring, grooming, head bunting, rubbing, encircling tails, and more. Being in a relationship with a human, I explored the importance and necessity of understanding and expressing gratitude.

For starters, I had a wonderful mother who cared for me and taught me to care as well.

I was with my mother when she breathed her last. As I tried to protect her as she died, no vehicle struck either or us. Humans did show some respect for us by driving around us. I didn't appreciate that then.

The fan belt didn't totally remove my foot or kill me. Despite what seemed like excessive blood loss, I didn't bleed to death. I was able to manage for more time than I had expected given the severity of my injury.

In my vulnerable state no dog, cat, or raccoon managed to attack or dispatch me. They may have been laughing too much at my behaviors to bother to really go after me, but irrespective—

Two humans, whom I had summarily dismissed because of my perception of their "questionable" actions, had shown a positive interest in my well-being. They tried to save me. But I didn't give them the benefit of the doubt and wouldn't let them.

An ill and dying mama dog generously took me in. She kept me warm, saving me for another day. She also gave me the opportunity to share my warmth and appreciative attention with her. Maybe that was the only true attention she had ever had. Maybe my behavior gave her a better send-off, one she truly deserved.

A caring human spotted and rescued me when I was on my last legs (literally) and sure to expire at the side of an icy road.

And last but surely not least, a kind and skillful veterinarian knew precisely what to do. He watchfully assisted me through my long, painful recovery and the successful reconstruction of my foot.

Amazingly, I had survived my life, with its physical and emotional trauma and torment. But more importantly I had exchanged the unrelenting cruelty of homelessness for a permanent home. I had received a new life filled with soothing touch, love, and catnip. Through my journey, I learned about life, myself, humans, and my expectations about them all.

With all that in mind I dedicate this memoir with love to my Special Friend whose unwavering compassion, respect, and actions literally and figuratively transformed me. She gave my life a special purpose which I relish. She helped me in every way navigate the hazardous uncharted waters from "footless" to "footloose and fancy free." Thank you!

* * *

ABOUT THE AUTHOR

Signe A. Dayhoff, PhD, is a social psychologist from Boston University with post-graduate training in counseling, emotional intelligence, and positive psychology. For over 30 years she has been a cognitive-behaviorist, coach, and author, specializing in increasing confidence and interpersonal communication skills and alleviating social anxiety.

An applied feline behaviorist and cat rescue volunteer, she is kitty-mom to 20-plus senior and disabled cats. She consults on improving human-cat communication and relationships.

She has taught psychology at Boston University, University of Massachusetts, and Framingham State College and has done research at Massachusetts Institute of Technology, Fairview State Hospital (aka, Fairview Developmental Center), and Scripps Clinic and Research Foundation.

She is author of eighteen books: *Remarkable Tales of Cats Who Whisper To Humans; Attracting and Dating the Wrong Men: Tips and Insights to Free Yourself; What Faust the Dancing Cat Taught Me; Growing Up "Unacceptable"—How Katharine Hepburn Rescued Me; How Insiders Get Jobs: 6-Mini-Course Series; Scared of Your Boss? Smash Through Your Fear Now; Promote Myself? I'd Rather Eat Worms!; How to Speak Without Fear Small Talk Course;* 2nd Ed. of *Diagonally-Parked in a Parallel Universe: Working Through Social Anxiety; Create Your Own Career Opportunities; Get The Job You Want;* and *Decision Making For Managers.* And she contributed to David Riklan's *101 Great Ways to Improve Your Life (Vol. 2)* and Steven J. Bennett's *Executive Chess: Creative Problem Solving by 45 of America's Top Business Leaders and Thinkers.*

Kindle and Paperback Books:
http://effectivenessplus.com/books

Confidence/Interpersonal Communication Skills Coaching:
http://effectivenessplus.com/coaching

www.ingramcontent.com/pod-product-compliance
Lightning Source LLC
Chambersburg PA
CBHW060649030426
42337CB00017B/2529